"Never, never, and never again shall it be that this beautiful land

will again experience the oppression of one by another . . ."

The Nelson Mandela Foundation is thanked for its support and advice.

Abridgement and illustrations copyright © 2009 by Macmillan
Published by Flash Point, an imprint of Roaring Brook Press
Roaring Brook Press is a division of Holtzbrinck Publishing Holdings Limited Partnership
175 Fifth Avenue, New York, New York 10010
www.roaringbrookpress.com
Published in Great Britain by Macmillan Children's Books, London
All rights reserved

Illustrations by Paddy Bouma
Text abridged by Chris van Wyk

Image on page 7 courtesy of Tom Stoddart Archive, Getty Images
The illustrator would like to thank Carin Matz for the use of her photograph on which the illustration
on page 53 is based, and also the Mayibuye Centre for their help with the image research.

Abridged from the book LONG WALK TO FREEDOM by Nelson Mandela
Copyright © Nelson Rolihlahla Mandela 2009

Cataloging-in-Publication Data is on file at the Library of Congress
ISBN: 978-1-59643-566-7

Roaring Brook Press books are available for special promotions and premiums.
For details contact: Director of Special Markets, Holtzbrinck Publishers.

First Edition September 2009
Printed in June 2009 in Singapore by Tien Wah Press
1 3 5 7 9 8 6 4 2

NELSON MANDELA
Long Walk to Freedom

Abridged by **CHRIS VAN WYK** · Illustrated by **PADDY BOUMA**

Rb.
Flash
Point

ROARING BROOK PRESS · NEW YORK

AFRICA

SOUTH
AFRICA

BOTSWANA

LIMPOPO

PRETORIA

NORTH WEST

JOHANNESBURG

SOWETO

GAUTENG

ALEXANDRA

MPUMALANGA

NAMIBIA

SWAZILAND

FREE STATE

KWAZULU-
NATAL

BLOEMFONTEIN

HOWICK

LESOTHO

DURBAN

SOUTH AFRICA

NORTHERN CAPE

UMTATA

CLARKEBURY
SCHOOL

QUNU

EASTERN CAPE

MVEZO

MQHEKEZWENI

FORT BEAUFORT
HEALDTOWN
COLLEGE

EAST LONDON

WESTERN CAPE

UNIVERSITY OF
FORT HARE

ROBBEN ISLAND

CAPE TOWN

PORT ELIZABETH

POLLSMOOR PRISON

My name is Nelson Mandela. I live in South Africa, a beautiful country on the tip of Africa. Today South Africa is a democracy. That means all adults vote to choose who they want to run the country. But it was not always like this.

When I was born, South Africa was ruled by white people only. As I grew older, I began to see that this was not fair. I wanted to change this way of government so everyone had a say. My friends and I called this the struggle for freedom. The struggle lasted many years, and I was one of the fighters. This is my story . . .

Long, long ago, white Europeans crossed the seas to South Africa. They fought over the land, and they also fought the tribes of people already living there, such as the Xhosas, the Zulus, and the Tswanas.

Hundreds of years later, I was born into the Thembu tribe, one of many tribes that made up the Xhosa nation. I entered the world in the tiny village of Mvezo, in the beautiful Eastern Cape, on July 18, 1918.

My father was a Thembu chief, a leader of our people. He named me Rolihlahla, which in Xhosa means "troublemaker." Did he believe I would grow up to be a troublemaker? I don't think so. Nobody knew what lay ahead of me.

When I was a young boy, we moved from Mvezo to the nearby village of Qunu, and I began herding our family's sheep and goats. Those were happy days. My friends and I swam in the rivers, stole honey from beehives, and played stick fighting—a Xhosa boy's favorite sport.

When I turned seven, my father decided to send me to school. It was a mission school, built by Europeans who had come to South Africa to spread Christianity. No one in my family had been to school before. I didn't have fancy clothes, but my father took a pair of his old trousers and cut them off at the knee. I used a piece of string as a belt. But the school wasn't fancy, either—it had only one classroom. None of the pupils wore better clothes, so I fitted right in.

Our teacher gave us new names. Mine was Nelson. Nelson? At that time, the English ruled our country, so our teacher thought we should all have English names. It sounded very strange at first, but I soon got used to it.

I was learning at school, but I was learning at home as well. My mother told me stories from long ago, full of wise lessons about being kind to others.

My father taught me to be a brave Xhosa boy. I wanted to grow up to be just like him. Sometimes I even rubbed ashes onto my hair to make it gray, like his.

But after my ninth birthday, my life changed. My father grew ill and died. My mother took me to live with my father's friend, Chief Jongintaba, in the nearby village of Mqhekezweni. Uncle Jongi was the acting king of the Thembus and was a very important man. He had an automobile and lived in a big house called the Great Place. It was an exciting new experience for me! My mother still came to visit me, though, and I was always happy to see her.

Although I missed Qunu, I loved my new life. Uncle Jongi's son, Justice, was a few years older than me, and we became best friends. We rode horses and plowed his father's fields together. We had a lot of fun!

But life was not all about riding horses. When I was sixteen, Uncle Jongi sent me to Clarkebury boarding school. In those days, many boys and girls did not finish their schooling, but my uncle believed education was important. Three years later, I joined Justice at Healdtown, the biggest school for Africans in the country. This is where I completed my high-school education.

At the age of twenty-one, I enrolled at
Fort Hare, a university for black students
in the Eastern Cape. Uncle Jongi bought me
a new suit to wear. It was very different
from the cut down trousers I had worn
when I went to school. I felt very grown-up!

Young black people from all over the
country came to study at Fort Hare. It was
the first time I had met people from other
tribes, such as Sothos, Zulus, and Tswanas.

I made new friends, including a clever
young student named Oliver Tambo.
Although we didn't know it then, Oliver
and I were to become very important
in each other's lives.

I worked hard at university but I had fun, too. I took up running, boxing, and ballroom dancing. One night, my friends and I snuck out to a dance hall. We thought we were very daring—until we met our teacher!

But suddenly, my student days were cut short. I was elected to sit on the Student Council, but only twenty-five students had voted. Most did not vote because the council could not change the thing that concerned them the most—the bad cafeteria food. I told the Principal that I would not sit on the council without the students' support. He was very angry and threatened to expel me, but I wouldn't change my mind. I never went back to university. Was I living up to my name of "troublemaker"?

Back at the Great Place, Uncle Jongi soon had other plans for me and Justice. He told us we were to be married, and he had already picked a wife for each of us. We were shocked! We didn't want to get married, and so we decided to run away to Johannesburg.

Johannesburg was more than four hundred miles away. It was known to all Xhosa people as Egoli, the Place of Gold. There we would find jobs and make new lives. It was an adventure, and we set off full of hope and excitement for the future, toward the twinkling lights of the big city.

The city was bigger than we could ever have imagined. Everywhere we looked there were people, shops, and cars. But those fancy shops and expensive cars belonged to white people. Most black people were poor.

I went to live in Alexandra township, just outside the city, where the tiny houses had no electricity or running water and the roads were just dusty paths. Life was hard in Alexandra, but it became home to me.

Justice stayed in Johannesburg for a while. But after a few years, Uncle Jongi died and Justice returned to the Eastern Cape to take over as chief.

I met many new people, but one of my best friends was Walter Sisulu. Walter and his family lived in Orlando West, Soweto, a black township near Johannesburg. I looked up to Walter. Like me, he was from the Eastern Cape, but he had been in Johannesburg longer and knew a lot about the city's people and places.

I spent a lot of time at the Sisulus' home. It was there I met Evelyn Mase, a young nurse and relative of the Sisulus. We fell in love and got married. We had two sons and two daughters, but one daughter did not live long. Sadly, Evelyn and I soon parted, but I remained close to my sons, Thembekile and Makgatho, and to my daughter, Makaziwe.

At the Sisulus', I also met my old friend Oliver Tambo again. We were both studying law, and in 1952, we set up the first black law firm in South Africa.

But there was another way we could try to improve the lives of black people. Ever since white people had come to South Africa, they had ruled black people. My friend Walter was a member of the African National Congress, or ANC, which had been fighting for the freedom of black people to rule themselves. Oliver and I joined, too, and, at Walter's home, we wondered how we could make the government take notice.

In 1944, we formed the ANC Youth League and planned to get thousands of young black people to join. We would protest peacefully by marching through the streets and demanding our freedom. We would not be ignored.

In 1948, the government started passing
laws that introduced apartheid, which
divided black and white people into
separate groups. White people lived
in suburbs while black people lived in
townships. The government also built
separate schools, churches, and movie
theaters for black and for white people.
There were even separate entrances to
post offices and shops.

All black people more than sixteen years
old had to carry a passbook showing who
we were, and where we worked and lived.
If we were found without our passbook, we
would be thrown into prison.

Apartheid was a cruel system. It classified every person in South Africa according to race, for example, as "black," "colored," or "white," and controlled the lives of those who were not white. It made me and my ANC comrades angry. In 1952, we led a protest called the Defiance Campaign, calling on black people to ignore the "Whites Only" entrances in post offices, shops, and trains. More than 250 people were arrested but thousands joined in.

The government didn't drop its apartheid laws, but the ANC now had many more members. We were getting stronger. The government banned me from attending ANC meetings or protesting against apartheid, but I went on working for the ANC in secret.

It was not only black people who were against apartheid. Thousands of colored, Indian, and white South Africans were against it, too. In the early 1950s, many of these different groups joined together to form the Congress Alliance. Then, in 1955, the ANC and the other members of the Congress Alliance met in Kliptown, near Johannesburg, to draw up the Freedom Charter. The meeting was called the Congress of the People, and the charter was a promise to fight for freedom and democracy for all South Africans. It began . . .

THE FREEDOM CHARTER

We the people of South Africa, declare for all our country and the world to know: That South Africa belongs to all who live in it, black and white . . .

The government did not like the charter and arrested 156 Congress members, including Oliver, Walter, and me. We were charged with planning to destroy the government. The trial lasted four long years, but in the end, we were found not guilty.

During that time, I fell in love again. Winnie Madikizela was a social worker and a member of the ANC. We got married in 1958 and had two daughters, Zenani and Zindzi.

In 1960, during our trial, a tragedy happened that shocked the world.

In Sharpeville, near Johannesburg, five thousand people marched to a police station to protest against having to carry passbooks. They were not armed, yet still the police fired guns at them.

Sixty-nine people were killed and four hundred were injured.

After Sharpeville, the government banned the ANC and other organizations fighting for freedom. They did not want to share South Africa with black people. Our peaceful marches had not worked, but we were not giving up. We decided that the only way to get our freedom was to fight the government in the same way as they were fighting us—with guns.

The ANC formed an army that we called Umkhonto we Sizwe, which in Xhosa means "The Spear of the Nation." I was sent abroad on a secret mission to ask other countries to help us fight apartheid. I also went to train as a soldier.

In 1962, I returned to South Africa, using a false passport and calling myself David Motsamayi. I stayed in hiding for many months while the police searched everywhere for Nelson Mandela. . . .

Then, one day in August, I was stopped in my car and arrested. I was sentenced to five years in prison for leaving the country illegally and for inciting workers to strike. Later, the police also arrested a group of my comrades, including my old friend Walter Sisulu. Just nine months into my five-year sentence, I was told I would stand trial again. We were all charged with planning to overthrow the government. If we were found guilty, we could be sentenced to death.

The trial began in October 1963, and in April 1964 I spoke in defense of us all. I told the court that the ANC was a peaceful organization, but because the government had banned it, we had no peaceful way to protest. We had been imprisoned and even killed. This is why we had to fight back with guns. I said, "I have cherished the ideal of a democracy in which all persons live together in harmony. . . . It is an ideal for which I am prepared to die."

Eight of us were found guilty, but we were not sentenced to death. Instead, we were told we would spend the rest of our lives in prison. Life in prison! Would I ever see my wife, mother, and children again?

We were taken to Robben Island, a prison off the coast of Cape Town. All except our comrade Denis Goldberg. Of the eight of us, he was the only white person and had to serve his sentence at a different prison.

On Robben Island, my cell was so tiny that when I lay down on my sleeping mat, my feet and hands could touch opposite walls. I was given some thin blankets and a bucket for a toilet. This cell was to be my home.

I tried to stay hopeful, but it wasn't easy. At first, we were allowed only two visitors a year and just two letters. Before we were given them, the letters were read by a prison guard who blacked out anything he thought we shouldn't know about.

Twice I received bad news from home. First, I was told my mother had died. Then my eldest son, Thembekile, was killed in a car crash. When I got that news, I spent the whole day in my cell thinking about him and the rest of my family. It was one of the saddest days of my life.

We were not allowed radios or newspapers.
Weeks, months, years went by without us
knowing what was happening in the world.
One day, I saw that a warden had left
his newspaper lying on a chair. It was too
tempting. I grabbed the paper and began
reading it. I was caught and locked in a
room for three days with no food and only
rice water to drink as a punishment.

Slowly the years passed. Five years . . .
ten . . . twenty. I no longer needed ashes
to make my hair gray!

But outside the prison, the fight for
freedom went on.

Even though the ANC was banned in South Africa, it continued outside the country. Oliver Tambo was living abroad and was now ANC president. Many governments around the world began to support us.

In the 1980s, the ANC launched the "Release Mandela" campaign, asking people all over the world to put pressure on the South African government to release me and my fellow prisoners and to allow the ANC back in. Thousands of people signed the petition.

Then, in March 1982, Walter, a few other prisoners, and I were moved to Pollsmoor prison near Cape Town. Was this a sign that things were beginning to change? Should I dare to hope our struggle for freedom was coming to an end? The government and I began secret talks about peace.

In 1988, I was moved again to a prison called Victor Verster, but instead of a cell, I was given a cottage with a bedroom, a kitchen, and a swimming pool!

The government and I continued our talks, and in December 1989, I met with President de Klerk and we talked about a new South Africa. Things began to move very quickly.

Back in October 1989, a number of my former Robben Island comrades had been released, including Walter Sisulu. Then, on February 2, 1990, and two months after our meeting, President de Klerk stunned the world by announcing that I was to be released, along with all other political prisoners. He said it was time to talk about a new country.

On February 11, 1990, I walked out of prison. Twenty-seven years of my life had passed since I was first taken to Robben Island. But the long walk to freedom was almost over.

It was wonderful to hold my lovely wife Winnie in my arms, to see my four beautiful children—now grown up, and to hear my grandchildren laugh and call me Granddad!

Every day our Soweto home was filled with laughter and tears of joy as friends I hadn't seen in twenty-seven years came to welcome me home.

After our release, there was a lot of work to be done. The ANC and the government began to speak about peace, and about a South Africa that would be shared by all its people, black and white.

And on April 27, 1994, millions of people, young and old, streamed out of their homes to vote. It was the first time ever for black people, and they joined white people to vote for a new South Africa. It was a wonderful day!

In May 1994, I became the first president
of South Africa to be elected by all
the people. I was seventy-five years old.
My journey to freedom had ended.

But a new journey has now begun—a journey to build a new South Africa. We must join hands and say we are one country, one nation, one people, marching together into the future. A future in which people of all colors will learn to live in peace.

TIMELINE

1918 Nelson Mandela is born at Mvezo on July 18 and named Rolihlahla.

1925 He goes to a Methodist mission school and is renamed Nelson by his teacher.

1927 His father, Henry Gadla Mphakanyiswa, dies. Mandela goes to live with Chief Jongintaba Dalindyebo.

1934 Mandela goes to Clarkebury Boarding Institute.

1937 Mandela goes to Healdtown, the Wesleyan College at Fort Beaufort.

1939 Mandela enrolls at University College of Fort Hare.

1940 Mandela leaves Fort Hare after refusing to sit on the Student Council.

1941 Mandela runs away to Johannesburg.

1944 Mandela joins the ANC and helps to form the Youth League. He marries Evelyn Mase.

1948 The first laws of apartheid are introduced.

1952 Mandela opens South Africa's first black law firm with Oliver Tambo. The ANC and the SAIC launch the Defiance Campaign.

1955 The Freedom Charter is drawn up at the Congress of the People.

1956 Mandela is charged with treason along with 155 others. His four-year court case begins.

1958 Mandela divorces Evelyn Mase. He marries Winnie Madikizela.

1960 The Sharpeville massacre occurs. The government bans the ANC.

1961 Mandela's treason trial ends. He is found not guilty. The ANC forms an army.

1962 Mandela is sent to get support from other countries. He is arrested again on his return to South Africa. He is sentenced to five years for leaving the country illegally and inciting workers to strike.

1963 Nine months into his sentence, Mandela is told he will stand trial again.

1964 Mandela is found guilty of sabotage, along with Walter Sisulu, Ahmed Kathrada, Raymond Mhlaba, Govan Mbeki, Denis Goldberg, Elias Motsoaledi, and Andrew Mlangeni. He is sentenced to life in prison and sent to Robben Island.

1969 Mandela's son, Thembekile, dies in a car accident.

1980–1981 Thousands of people sign the "Release Mandela" petition.

1982 Mandela is moved to Pollsmoor prison.

1988 Mandela is moved to Victor Verster prison.

1989 Five of the men who were convicted alongside Mandela are released: Sisulu, Kathrada, Mhlaba, Motsoaledi, and Mlangeni. (Goldberg had been released earlier in 1985, and Mbeki in 1987.)

1990 Mandela is released from prison.

1994 Mandela votes for the first time in his life in South Africa's first democratic election. He is elected as President of South Africa.

GLOSSARY

African National Congress (ANC): An organization formed in 1912 by those who believed that all Africans should be free to vote to choose their own leaders. The ANC led the fight to end apartheid.

apartheid: A system, introduced in 1948, that classified and separated black, colored and Indian people from white people in South Africa. Under the laws of apartheid, only white people could vote, and the lives of black people were strictly controlled. The word *apartheid* means "apartness."

charter: A document which states a group's ideas, beliefs, and demands.

comrades: A word sometimes used to describe people who share the same ideas and beliefs.

Congress of the People: A group of different organizations that met in Kliptown, Johannesburg, in 1955 to write down their beliefs and demands for a new South Africa. The groups included the ANC, representatives from the white COD (the Congress of Democrats), Indian people from the SAIC (South African Indian Congress), and colored people from the SACPO (South African Colored People's Organization). The Freedom Charter was agreed to at the Congress of the People.

de Klerk: Frederik Willem de Klerk was president of South Africa from 1989 to 1994. In 1990, he ended the ban on the ANC and ordered the release of Mandela. Under his leadership, the government reversed the last of the apartheid laws. De Klerk and Mandela were awarded the Nobel Peace Prize in 1993.

elected: To get the most votes of all the people running for office.

government: A political group who are in power and run a country.

inciting: To strongly encourage somebody to break rules.

overthrow: To defeat or destroy.

petition: A written request that is signed by all those who agree with it.

political prisoners: People who have been put into prison for fighting against or disagreeing with the government.

protest: To object strongly to something.

sabotage: To deliberately damage something.

township: An area set aside in South African cities for black people to live. White people lived in the richer suburbs.

trial: The hearing of a case in court.

tribe: A group of people with a shared language and culture, often from the same area.

warden: A person who works in a prison.

Xhosa nation: A group made up of many different tribes who have lived in the south eastern region of South Africa since at least the eleventh century, and who speak the same language.